Advanced Migrations with Django and South

A Developer's Guide

Table of Contents

Chapter 1. Introduction

Welcome to a Special Report uniquely designed with developers in mind: "Advanced Migrations with Django and South: A Developer's Guide." This comprehensive roadmap is meticulously curated to untangle the complex web of database migration processes involving Django, a high-level Python web framework, and South, a Django database migration tool. Delving beyond the surface-level treatments found in basic tutorials, this report treats both the fundamental concepts and the hidden intricacies with the sober precision required by advanced technical topics. However, don't be daunted. It demystifies advanced migration techniques, empowering you to handle intricate scenarios with confidence. This definitive guide beckons you to adventure—the journey, while challenging, promises masterful command over Django migrations. Strap in, it's time to morph into the Django and South expert you aspire to be.

Chapter 2. Overview of Database Migrations and Their Importance

Database migration is a term you will frequently encounter while dealing with web applications, particularly those that rely extensively on database interaction. While it keeps a distinct importance for all, understanding it is preeminent for developers who work with Django and South. The primary concern it addresses revolves around evolving your database schema to line up with the changes in the application schema over its lifecycle.

2.1. The Concept of Database Migration

Establishing a clear understanding of database migration is crucial before we delve into the practical application. In simple terms, database migration refers to the process of moving data from one type of database to another, or changing the database's structure itself. While migration may seem to be a simple 'move,' it is not equivalent to copying your data from one place to another—it involves a series of well-orchestrated processes that ensure data integrity, accuracy, and reliability before, during, and after the migration process.

To break it down further, migrations in Django are like a version control system for your database schema. If you are acquainted with Git, you would know the concept of commits. Similarly, in Django, a migration is akin to a 'commit' for your database schema. Each migration file corresponds to a specific change in your database schema, allowing it to coexist with your actual application codebase.

2.2. Significance of Database Migration

The role of migrations can't be understated for a variety of reasons.

1. Maintaining Consistency: Database migrations help maintain consistency between the actual database schema and the Django's models' schema representing it. As changes are made to models, migrations facilitate reflecting these changes in the database schema.

2. Deployments: They also play an essential role during codebase deployment. As the codebase is updated, migrations handle updating the database to match the current state of models in the application.

3. Versioning: In essence, migrations form a history (or versioning system) of your database. They enable you to iterate and roll-back changes made to your database schema should things go haywire.

4. Collaboration: On a collaborative level, migrations help multiple developers work on different aspects of the project simultaneously without worrying about conflicting changes to the database. Every developer makes their migrations, and Django manages to apply them in the correct order, resolving dependencies.

2.3. Types of Migrations

In the realm of Django and South, there are primarily two types of migrations:

1. *Schema Migrations:* These are the typical types associated with the term 'migration'. It alters the database structure (often referred to as schema). It involves operations like creating a table

(CreateModel), deleting a table (DeleteModel), or changing field properties (AlterField).

2. *Data Migrations:* As the name suggests, this type encompasses transformations that temper with the data but not the schema—like changing the value of a field for all instances in a given model.

2.4. Evolution, the Catalyst of Migration

The necessity of database migrations arise primarily due to evolutionary updates during the development life cycle. The process typically follows this pattern: 1. Start with creating Django models. 2. Generate and apply a migration based on the changes detected in your models. 3. For every change in your models, generate a new migration that Django knows how to apply.

This cycle repeats as new changes come in during development.

2.5. Database Migration: Not Always a Cakewalk

While Django's migration system is designed to handle most complexities, some scenarios may pose substantial challenges. It could be due to:

1. Significant structural changes that might result in data loss.

2. Complex dependencies between several apps' migrations.

Handling such intricate scenarios requires a profound understanding of South and Django migrations, their internals, and their optimal usage. An in-depth understanding of the migration process is not just useful but essential for advanced developers using Django, which leads us to why one needs to understand advanced migrations with Django and South.

In the end, learning how to do database migrations effectively and correctly makes you a confident, capable, and flexible Django developer, ready to handle real-world challenges that web development might throw at you. It's no longer a mysterious or intimidating process, but rather an empowering toolset in your development process.

In the following chapters, we will demystify Django's migration system further and discuss in detail how to use South for performing advanced migrations. Buckle up as we prepare to explore migrations' intricacies, from simple implementations to understanding how to grapple with complex scenarios. Happy coding!

Chapter 3. Introduction to Django: A High-Level Python Web Framework

With roots dating back to the late 2000s, Django emerged as a high-level Python web framework offering a rich set of components designed to help developers create secure and maintainable web applications. Known for its flexible and pluggable architecture, Django simplifies the construction of complex, database-driven websites.

The brilliance of Django lies in its design philosophy, emphasizing the simplicity of Pythonic conventions coupled with quick development times. "Don't Repeat Yourself (DRY)" and "Rapid Development" have become Django's guiding principles. The framework allows developers to focus more on writing the app without needing to reinvent the wheel.

3.1. Django's Architecture

Django adopts the architectural pattern known as Model-View-Controller (MVC). However, Django's interpretation of MVC might be slightly different from the classical one; it's often referred to as the Model-View-Template (MVT) architecture. Let's take a closer look at these components:

Models: A model is the definitive source of truth about your data. It contains basic fields and behaviors of the data you are storing. Each model maps to a single database table.

Views: A view is a Python function that takes a web request and returns a web response. Each view processes data and dispatches a template with context data.

Templates: Templates are designer-friendly syntax for rendering the information to be presented to the user. It decouples design and content rendering from Python scripting.

3.2. Django's ORM

One of the most influential and appreciated features of Django is its Object Relational Mapper (ORM). The Django ORM allows developers to interact with their database like they would with SQL. In other words, it's a way to create, retrieve, update, and delete records in your database using Python. ORM provides a high-level, abstracted and pythonic way to interact with your data.

ORMs provide an application-level data model, abstracting and encapsulating databases' structures via Python classes and functions.

In Django, each model is a Python class that subclasses `django.db.models.Model` and each attribute of the class represents a database field. Django's ORM allows for easy database manipulation directly from Python code, avoiding the need for extensive SQL scripts.

3.3. Rapid Development

"Django: The web framework for perfectionists with deadlines" is Django's tagline. Django aims to make developers' lives more comfortable by providing robust templates, form handling, authentication, and other essential aspects of web development right out of the box. Developers can focus their efforts on building the unique parts of the application without having to worry about these fundamental building blocks.

And whenever the need arises, Django's offerings can be easily overridden or extended, which ensures that the framework can still meet the needs of the most complex websites.

3.4. Django's Migrations

Migrations help in propelling a Django project forward by facilitating changes to the database schema without losing data. They are designed to be mostly automatic, but you'll need to know when to run them and the common problems you might run into.

Example:

```
python manage.py makemigrations yourappname
```

This command generates the SQL commands necessary to apply or unapply the migration. Migrations make it easy to change the database schema, which evolves as the application's requirements change.

3.5. Security

Django is highly regarded for its robust security mechanisms — it effectively handles common security issues like SQL injection, Cross-Site Scripting (XSS), Cross-Site Request Forgery (CSRF), and Clickjacking. In addition to these, Django also provides secure password hashing that shields applications from brute force and rainbow table attacks.

3.6. Summary

The elegance of Django as a high-level Python web framework is indisputable: it's powerful and flexible yet maintains a high standard of convenience. Whether you're working on a small personal project or a complex web application serving millions of users, Django offers all the tools you need for elegant, efficient and security-conscious Python web development. With its robust and ever-growing

community, Django is an excellent choice for developers of any skill
level.

Chapter 4. Unpacking South: Django's Essential Migration Tool

In the ever-evolving universe of web development, database migration is no less than a critical survival skill. South, Django's essential migration tool, is an invaluable companion for any developer poised to grapple with the complex terrain of Django-based data migrations. Globally recognized for its robustness and reliability, South essentially manifests as a programmer's machete, forging paths through the dense forest of Django database variations and maintenance.

4.1. Inside out: A Close Look at South

Let us first dissect the tool to know it better. South is a Django project component intended to handle schema and data migrations. Its structural anatomy is straightforward; South is not dissimilar to Django applications, comprised of models, migrations, and handlers.

Its key components are:

- `Migration History`: This is essentially a record of all migrations that have occurred, keeping track of the versions of your database.

- `Migrations Directory`: This directory houses the Python files, which detail how South should act when updating or reverting your database schema.

- `Autodetection`: It is an advanced feature of South that automatically identifies any modifications made to models and prepares a migration for them.

With these core components, South equips you with the ability to initiate, control, and reverse migrations effortlessly.

4.2. An Arsenal for Every Need: South's Tools

The power of South resides not just in its super-structural design, but also in the extensive toolkit it provides.

- `schemamigration`: This is the tool for generating migration files based on the changes detected in your model. Options available include `'--auto'`, which generates a migration to match the current models' state, and `'--initial'` to generate a migration to match the initial state of a model.

- `datamigration`: This facilitates the creation of a blank migration file, providing flexibility when you need to alter data in ways that South cannot auto-detect.

- `migrate`: This under-the-hood powerhouse is what applies or unapplies migrations.

- `graphmigrations`: It visualizes your migrations and their dependencies, an often overlooked but crucial aspect of maintaining complex databases.

These tools collectively empower Django developers to intuitively interact with databases, thus pushing the boundaries of precision, control, and efficiency in web development.

4.3. Setting Sail: Integrating South in Your Project

South melds seamlessly into Django projects. It can be added to `INSTALLED_APPS` in your Django's settings.py file. You have to run `python manage.py syncdb` initially to create the requisite tables in your database. This primes your Django project for South-led migration adventures.

4.4. Smooth Sailing: Handling Schema Migrations with South

South truly shines when it comes to schema migrations. The journey begins with running `python manage.py schemamigration appname --initial`, where 'appname' is your application's name. This command generates a migration script for your model. Subsequently, the `python manage.py migrate appname` brings the migration to life, applying it to your database. Any further changes necessitating migrations are effortlessly managed by South's `--auto` option.

4.5. Navigating Choppy Waters: Advanced Migrations & South

South's adaptability to complex migrations is praiseworthy. Let's say you require changes that alter data in a way South cannot auto-detect. This situation calls for data migrations. To use the `python manage.py datamigration appname migrationname` command, writing up a few Python methods in the created file does the job.

For instances when you need to make drastic model changes that South does not natively support, such as renaming a model or field, manual migrations become a recourse. An experienced hand combined with appropriate use of South's rich toolkit can facilitate such intricate tasks.

4.6. Pirates Beware: Dealing with Migration Conflicts

Migration conflicts can be challenging, but South has you covered. In case of conflicts, `./manage.py migrate appname zero` would help unravel the migrations, moving you back to a safe state, ready to embark on a fresh migration journey.

By understanding and embracing South as a dynamic migration tool, you contribute towards seamless, efficient, and DRY (Don't Repeat Yourself) coding - a desirable aspiration for any committed Django developer. Let your journey with South commence, so you may conquer the mountainous terrains of Django migrations with unmatched expertise.

Chapter 5. Starting with Basics: First Steps in Django Migrations

Django migrations are a crucial aspect of managing schema changes and dataset alterations in your applications. Before we begin the intricate process, it's essential to ensure we have Django and South installed properly on your development environment. If you've not done this yet, you can use pip, a package manager for Python. Here's how you can install Django:

```
$ pip install django
```

Similarly, install South using pip:

```
$ pip install South
```

Upon successful installation, the next step is to create a new Django project. You can use Django's `startproject` command.

```
$ django-admin startproject my_project
```

This is your first initiation into the Django environment. The `startproject` command creates a new Django project in a directory called `my_project`. It provides you with a host of automatically generated files that constitute the skeleton of a Django project.

5.1. Working with Django Models

With your new Django project set up, navigate into the project directory (`my_project`) and create a new application. Django encourages application modularity, meaning a single project can house multiple applications.

```
$ python manage.py startapp my_app
```

This command would create a new application `my_app` within your Django project. This application will contain its own `models.py` file, where you will define the application's database schema.

Chapter 6. Database Schema Creation in Django

A Django model is the single definitive source of information about your data. It contains the essential fields and behaviors of the data you're storing. Let's create our first model. Assuming we're building a simplistic blog, our `models.py` might look like this:

```python
from django.db import models

class Blog(models.Model):
    title = models.CharField(max_length=200)
    author = models.CharField(max_length=50)
    body = models.TextField()
    published = models.BooleanField(default=False)
```

In this `models.py` file, each attribute - `title`, `author`, `body`, `published` - represents a field in the database table `Blog`.

You should inform Django about the newly created application. In the settings file (`settings.py`), add `my_app` to your `INSTALLED_APPS`:

```python
INSTALLED_APPS = [
    ...,
    'my_app',
]
```

Chapter 7. Generate and Apply Migrations

Having added 'my_app' to your INSTALLED_APPS, you must make Django aware of the new database schema associated with it. Run the makemigrations command to create migrations for those changes:

```
$ python manage.py makemigrations my_app
```

Django would now create a new directory migrations/ within your app directory. This folder consists of migration scripts generated via makemigrations. Each script file represents a point in time for your application, and the changes made to your models.

To apply these migrations (create the relevant tables in the database), you must execute the migrate command:

```
$ python manage.py migrate
```

7.1. South: Migrating to another Database Schema

South provides a smooth transition for schema migrations in Django. It boasts features like consistent handling of schema migrations and the ability to roll back schema changes. Before diving into South, ensure South is added to your INSTALLED_APPS:

```
INSTALLED_APPS = [
    ...,
    'south',
```

```
    ...,
]
```

In South, a migration is a method of changing your database schema from one version to another. The process begins with the `schemamigration` command. We'll add a `created_date` field to our `Blog` model:

```
class Blog(models.Model):
    ...
    created_date =
models.DateTimeField(auto_now_add=True)
```

We then use `schemamigration` to create a schema migration script:

```
$ python manage.py schemamigration my_app --auto
```

The above command would create a new migration which adds the `created_date` field to the `Blog` model. The `--auto` option is used for automatically detecting changes to the models.

Next, apply the migration:

```
$ python manage.py migrate my_app
```

This final command merges the changes with your existing database schema. The schema now correctly mirrors the current state of your Django models.

South provides not just a more structured migration path than Django's built-in capabilities, but also provides additional features such as data and schema migration mix, dependencies between migrations, and named migrations.

The start into Django migrations and South is complete. Those were your first steps, now you are ready to tread onto the path that leads to more complex migrations scenarios. Because as your projects grow, so does the complexity of maintaining sync between your Django models and the database schema.

There might be moments when mistakes happen, and a migration turns out to be flawed. Thus, understanding rollback procedures is of critical importance. In the next chapter, we shall delve into the details of reversing migrations. As a preview, you would need to master South's `migrate` command, which not only applies migrations but can also unapply them, bringing your database schema back to a previous state. But more on this in the forthcoming chapter - until then, happy exploring!

Chapter 8. Beyond the Basics: Embracing Advanced Django Migrations

Before delving into an exhaustive exploration of advanced Django migrations, it is invaluable to have a refresher on the fundamentals. Migrations are Django's way of managing changes to your models (and consequently your database schema) - they are mainly comprised of the concepts of `makemigrations` and `migrate`.

Now, let's venture beyond these basics, immersing ourselves into the ocean of advanced Django migrations. The depths here comprise complex scenarios like database schema changes, handling dependencies between migrations, storing data before a destructive migration, using RunPython safely, and further topics.

8.1. Advanced Schema Editing

Django tries to make schema editing smooth with the `makemigrations` command generating automatic migrations. But there are cases where manual intervention is required.

When altering a Django model field's arguments, Django automatically manages it; however, renaming the model's field incurs complications. Django perceives this as removing the old field and creating a new one due to the loss of the old field's data.

To effectively rename model's field, you should:

1. Create a new field.

2. Create a data migration to copy data from the old field to the new one.

3. Remove the old field.

In the second step, creating a data migration would involve `RunPython` method (we will discuss this in detail later).

8.2. Managing Migration Dependencies

While working on a large project with multiple developers, migration dependencies can be a common problem. Django automatically creates a dependency on the previous migration when generating migrations. Generally, this works fine, but on large codebases with a large number of migrations, it could lead to conflicts.

Thankfully, Django provides an easy way to create dependencies between migrations and avoid conflicts via the `dependencies` attribute in the `Migration` class.

Example:

```python
class Migration(migrations.Migration):

    dependencies = [
        ('app_name', '0004_previous_migration'),
    ]
```

The above snippet implies that this migration will only run after the specified dependency migration has run.

8.3. Preserving Data during Destructive Migrations

There may be situations where data needs to be preserved before a destructive migration operation such as removing a model or a field. Several approaches include:

1. Writing a data migration to copy the required data to a temporary model or an existing model that will not be affected by the migration.

2. Exporting the data to an external source before the migration and then re-importing it.

8.4. Using RunPython Safely

Django provides the `RunPython` operation to execute Python code in migrations. It is a powerful tool that enables data transformations, complex schema changes, etc.

However, using `RunPython` in a migration must be undertaken with caution, as once a migration with `RunPython` is applied, undoing it can be complex.

When possible, providing a `reverse_code` function (which undoes what the `RunPython` operation does) is recommended. This function is executed when unapplying migrations.

8.5. Squashing Migrations

As the codebase matures, the migrations directory might get cluttered with hundreds of migration files, which slows down tests and deployments.

Django offers 'migration squashing' to remedy this. Squashing is the process of combining several existing migrations into one migration. The command is `python manage.py squashmigrations app_label start_migration_name end_migration_name`.

However, squashing should be undertaken judiciously, considering both the development phase and the deployment phase.

8.6. Performing Safe Database Schema Changes in Production

When deploying migrations to production, always ensure they are both backward and forward-compatible with the current live version of the application.

1. **Adding fields:** Always add new fields with null=True, as during the deployment, the old code might still be running and those code paths do not know about the new field.

2. **Removing fields:** Never remove a field that is still being used by the code. Always ensure that the code that refers to the field is removed and deployed, and then the field can be removed in a separate deployment.

3. **Renaming fields:** Like removing, renaming should be done in multiply deployments: first, add a new field and change the code to use it, then remove the old field in a separate deployment.

4. **Altering field types:** This operation is more complex as it depends on the database used and the type of change.

Moving beyond the basics of Django migrations proves to be a challenging but rewarding experience as it equips you with the dexterity needed to handle extensive Django applications. This intricate world, although complex, isn't to be feared, but to be explored, learned and mastered. As a Django developer, challenging migrations no longer need to be a stumbling block, but a stepping stone on your path to becoming a master developer.

Chapter 9. The Art of Rollbacks: Techniques for Undoing Migrations

In the world of database migrations, the ability to undo changes—known as a "rollback"— is crucial. Django and South provide support for this type of operation, but applying it correctly and efficiently requires know-how. This chapter will delve into the tips and tricks for successfully 'rolling back' migrations using Django and South.

9.1. Understanding Rollbacks

At its core, a rollback is the process of undoing changes that have been made to your database schema or data by a migration. It's a type of "undo" function that allows you to revert back to a previous state if something goes wrong during a migration or in the period following one.

In the context of Django and South, migrations are stored as Python files that include an `forwards` method for applying the migration and a `backwards` method for undoing it. These methods consist of procedural code that describes how to change the database schema and, sometimes, the data itself.

When a migration is run using `./manage.py migrate <appname>`, the `forwards` method is executed. If for any reason you need to revert that migration, Django and South gives you the option to run `./manage.py migrate <appname> <migrationname>`, which will execute the `backwards` method of the specified migration, essentially rolling back the migration.

9.2. Planning for Rollbacks

Before diving into the specifics of how to execute rollbacks, it is important to keep in mind that not all database operations can be easily undone. Some operations, like data deletions, cannot be reversed without a backup of the data. A good migration strategy should include comprehensive backup procedures, which will allow you to restore data when necessary.

Likewise, creating 'rollback-able' migrations is an art in itself. When writing the `backwards` method, you should ensure it adequately reverts the `forwards` methods' changes. To do this, you have to keep track of any destructive changes being made in the `forwards` method and provide an alternative for them in the `backwards` method.

9.3. Executing Rollbacks

If you have a series of migrations and want to revert to a specific state identified by a migration name, you can use the `migrate` command followed by the app name and the proper migration name. Let's say you have three migrations: 0001, 0002, and 0003, and you want to revert to state 0001. You would run:

```
./manage.py migrate myapp 0001
```

This command will execute the `backwards` methods of migration 0003 and 0002, in that order, and leave your database in the state described by migration 0001.

However, to rollback the last migration irrespective of its name, you can simply skip the migration name from the migrate command:

```
./manage.py migrate myapp
```

9.4. Rollbacks and Data Integrity

Rollbacks have the potential to be fraught with complications when it comes to data integrity. For instance, if a migration involved adding a column and the `forwards` method populated it with computed or fetched data, merely dropping the column in the `backwards` method results in data loss.

The safest way to handle this scenario is to keep the data until you are absolutely sure it's no longer needed.

To illustrate, let's consider a scenario where you added a column, computed some values, and populated it in the `forwards` method. In such circumstances, instead of just deleting the column in the `backwards` method, you may want to:

1. Create a new table that mirrors the structure of the existing table.

2. Move the records you want to keep from the existing table to this new table.

3. Rename (or drop and recreate, which can be faster but more dangerous) the existing table minus the column added earlier.

4. Move the records from the new table back to the actual one.

5. Delete the new table.

This approach ensures that, if there's a requirement to restore the removed data, it's available up until the last stage of the process.

9.5. Rollbacks and Zero Downtime

Rollbacks can be more challenging when considering zero downtime deployments. A rollback might be necessary during deployment if defects are found or if a database update fails for some reason.

In a system designed for zero downtime, both the previous and the new version of the application need to be capable of running concurrently. For this reason, any changes to the database schema must be made in a backwards-compatible way.

One method to achieve this is through the use of multi-phase deployments. A change that would be done in one deployment is instead done over two or more, with each deployment including a portion of the changes that maintain backwards compatibility, until all the changes have been applied.

Finally, it's important to keep track of your deployments and the order of your migrations. Maintaining a log of migrations can help detect anomalies or inconsistencies in the rollback process and help you address them before they become major issues.

As a Django developer, understanding and mastering rollbacks can be a boon in maintaining and ensuring the optimal working of your application's database. This technique serves as your safety net, ensuring that even in the face of unexpected migration issues, recovery and continuity of business processes are always within grasp. Undoubtedly, mastering the art of rollbacks is an essential tool in a developer's arsenal when working with Django and South migrations.

Chapter 10. Data Integrity and Migrations: Understanding Lossless Transition

Database integrity lies at the very heart of migration tasks. Failing to maintain integrity during migrations will result in data anomalies that could cause havoc in the system. While Django and South work together to generate the necessary SQL code, you as the developer need to be proactive and understand how they can ensure a lossless transition.

10.1. The Principle of Data Integrity

Data integrity refers to the overall completeness, accuracy, and consistency of data. It is about maintaining the fidelity of the data before, during, and after any changes or processes that affect the data, in this case, migrations. Even if the final stored value is correct, if the transition isn't accurate and complete, data integrity will be compromised.

During execution, migrations are atomic, meaning they are presented as a single unit of work, and they're either entirely completed or entirely rolled back. This integrity is maintained to prevent state inconsistency if a migration operation fails to complete.

10.2. The Constraints of Data Integrity

Constraints enforce the business rules on the data and help maintain the data integrity. Django provides several built-in constraints like unique_together, ForeignKey and OneToOneField, each of which plays a crucial role to enforce data integrity.

Moreover, South helps in maintaining the schema changes such that any changes in the constraints during migration retain database integrity.

10.3. South Avoids Data Anomalies

Data anomalies, in database parlance, typically fall into one of the three categories: update, deletion, and insertion. One of South's most significant advantages is how it tackles these potential anomalies.

South accomplishes this by creating custom migration methods, which are Python methods that the developer has the opportunity to override during the migration process. For instance, you could write a migration method to avoid the deletion anomaly where the associated data is removed when a particular record is deleted.

10.4. Ensuring Integrity amidst Changes in Data Types

When you change the field type involved in a migration, South will attempt to cast the existing values into the new datatype. However, there are scenarios where a simple cast operation fails to preserve the original data value. You need an explicit transformation function to ensure safe and accurate data conversion.

10.5. Integrity in Foreign Key Field Migrations

Foreign Key fields introduce their complexities when it comes to data integrity. South provides distinct methods to effectively deal with Foreign Key migrations while ensuring data integrity. You can apply unique indexes to the Foreign Key fields and utilize different strategies such as using NULL or Temporary values during migrations to preserve data integrity.

10.6. Dry Runs to Identify Potential Hitches

To preempt any hitches, South provides the `-n/--noinput` option to carry out a dry run of your migrations. This procedure is hugely beneficial for identifying any potential issues that may arise during the real process and providing an additional layer of assurance for data integrity.

10.7. Testing Migrations

Validation and testing of migrations take a central place in providing confidence in the migration process. It not only helps in keeping unforeseen bugs at bay but importantly, safeguards data integrity. Django's testing framework and the `south.tests` module come in handy in writing tests for your migrations.

Regular validation and testing are integral to maintaining data integrity during migrations. Errors in migrations can have far-reaching, often detrimental effects on an application's overall functionality, hence it's crucial to invest time and effort into this.

10.8. Restoring Integrity Post-Migration

Sometimes, despite best efforts, migrations tend to fail. Knowing how to restore the database integrity post a bad migration is a valuable skill. Tools like `db.migrate` and `db.rollback` in South prove quite handy for this purpose. An efficient backup strategy can also save you from potential disasters.

In conclusion, effective handling of data integrity and migrations is part art, part science. Django and South, through their robust and feature-rich ecosystem, offer an exciting canvas to paint this journey on. Kinesthetic knowledge gained through working with these tools will empower you to confidently maintain data integrity during the complex processes of migration, a skill indispensable in the world of databases.

Chapter 11. Advanced South Strategies: Optimizing Your Migrations

Before delving into the advanced strategies, it's crucial to understand the fundamental concepts of South migrations. For the most part, South provides a set of simple commands for creating new migrations and applying them, but behind the scenes, it's a robust tool with the power to deal with complex migration scenarios. Here we'll talk about some advanced South capabilities, from optimizing your migrations to dealing with potential errors.

11.1. Schema Altering Strategies

Optimizing the schema altering process is an essential part of efficient migrations strategy. South offers a group of high-level operations that allow developers to manipulate the schema without diving into SQL.

`startmigration` allows you manually set the dependencies and operations for your migrations, which can be optimized for performance. However, be aware that manual operations can increase the opportunity for mistakes. Handle with care.

`schemaeditor` provides a more automatic and less error-prone way to change the database schema. It offers advanced operations like `create_model`, `delete_model`, `add_field`, `delete_field`, `alter_field` and `rename_field`.

It's important to consider the database that's being used. For instance, PostgreSQL is great for managing complex operations, but MySQL might struggle with zero-downtime deployments due to its lack of transactional DDL (Data Definition Language). South is robust, but you need to consider these factors when making migrations more efficient.

11.2. Transformations and Data Migration

When dealing with database transformations, South offers two high-level operations which are `runpython` and `runsql`. When these operations mix with schema altering operations, it forms a complex data migration process that requires careful planning.

If you're having to transform the data with a new schema, consider splitting the transformation into different steps. Transform the data first to fit the new schema, then apply the schema migration.

For more complex operations, `runpython` might come in handy. This function allows developers to execute arbitrary Python code. This could mean populating the data in a new column based on the values from other fields, or even hitting an external API for data.

It's also worth mentioning `runsql`, which allows developers to execute raw SQL code. It's a powerful tool especially when dealing with heavy data transformations that require optimized SQL queries.

11.3. Dealing with Dependencies

While managing advanced migrations, dependencies between migrations become more intricate. Mismanaged dependencies could lead to fatal errors and database inconsistencies.

South provides two high-level operations for managing dependencies: `depends_on` and `needed_by`. Depends_on means that a migration is dependent on another migration to run first. Needed_by is just the opposite. Handle these dependencies with care, particularly when dealing with circular dependencies.

It's also possible to manage dependencies manually with the `startmigration` command, but keep in mind that it can increase the opportunity for mistakes due to its manual nature.

11.4. Managing Migration History

Knowing how to manage and manipulate migration history can be vital for advanced migration scenarios. South addresses this with `migrate` and `rollback` commands.

`Migrate` applies one or all migrations. You can roll back the applied migrations using `rollback` command. Use these commands wisely for rectifying failed migrations, applying migrations selectively and bypassing certain migrations in the deployment process.

Be aware that reversing a migration can potentially cause data loss if it includes an operation such as `DeleteModel` or `DeleteField`.

11.5. Error Handling and Trouble Shooting

South provides a set of commands and techniques to address common issues and special cases. By increasing your debugging skills, you can effectively intercept and address migration errors, thus strengthening the overall migration process.

`[django-admin.py] south_debug`; this command provides a detailed report of the entire migration history of your project, including migration status, dependencies, and related schema changes. Keep in mind that understanding the structure of the debug output will help you pinpoint issues more accurately.

Proceeding from these foundations and strategies, South becomes an even more powerful tool in your Django toolkit. With continuous practice, you'll find your comfort and skill with using South for your migrations increasing dramatically. Making the best of South involves learning a new way of thinking about migrations, and mastering advanced operations, troubleshooting techniques, and maintaining rigour and detail in your workflow. It's a challenging endeavor, but the rewards - a more efficient, reliable, and in-control process for evolving your Django projects' data layers - are well worth the effort. Continue exploring, learning, and creating with this powerful tool. Happy migrating!

Chapter 12. Troubleshooting: Solving Common Migration Hitches

In the throes of executing complex migration operations, modern developers occasionally stumble upon unexpected hitches. Problems may range from errors originating from database schema inconsistencies to those arising from neglecting Django requirement's peculiarities. To expedite your debugging process, we share a wellspring of accumulated wisdom on the most common stumbling blocks and how to effectively navigate around them.

12.1. Understanding Migration Errors

Before you can tackle a problem, you must first understand it. It's important to not just comprehend the particular error message you're seeing, but to familiarize yourself with the types of errors you're likely to encounter when doing migrations in Django with South.

12.1.1. Database errors

The most common form of migration errors are database errors. These arise when Django's ORM and your database schema are no longer compatible, often due to changes in your Django models. In these situations, an error pointing to a specific field or table is often case, as either no longer exists, or its data type has changed.

12.1.2. State errors

State errors occur when South loses track of the current state of your migrations. South relies on its own internal method for tracking the past migrations; consequently, if Django attempts to run a migration that South doesn't recognize or has forgotten, you will encounter a state error.

The most common type of state error is the `GhostMigrations` error, which occurs when Django thinks it needs to run migrations that South has already applied.

12.1.3. Circular Dependency

A circular dependency occurs when two or more migrations depend on each other, directly or indirectly. South struggles to apply these migrations, since it can't find an order of migrations that will satisfy all the dependencies.

12.2. Solving Database Errors

Database errors can sometimes be solved by simply altering the database schema manually, but this is not recommended due to the risk of losing or corrupting data. A safer approach is to use South's automated tools.

12.2.1. Correcting a removed field

If a field has been removed from a Django model but still exists in the database, you will encounter an error when Django tries to access this nonexistent field. You can correct such errors by creating a migration that removes the field from the database.

To do this, edit your Django model to reflect the current state of your database. After restoring the removed field, you can then create a migration:

```
$ python manage.py makemigrations your_app_name
```

Then apply it to update your database schema:

```
$ python manage.py migrate your_app_name
```

After running these commands, you should be able to remove the field from your models again safely, confident that it has been likewise removed from your database.

12.2.2. Correcting a changed data type

When a data type of a field in your Django model has changed but the database has not been updated yet, you will face a similar error. A migration can be created to alter the data type.

Like previous steps, first adjust your Django model to match what's present in your database. Then, make and apply the migration. After doing so, you can safely update your model to have the new data type, and create another migration for this change.

12.3. Solving State Errors

State errors are generally caused by the migration history getting out of step with the actual database schema. South includes some tools you can use to troubleshoot and fix these errors.

12.3.1. Resetting migrations

One way to solve this is by resetting your migrations. This will essentially tell South to forget all past migrations, which can be useful if your state has become too messy. Note that this is a drastic measure and should be employed sparingly, as you will have to manually reconcile your models and your database schema afterwards.

To clear all migrations for an app, run the South reset command:

```
$ python manage.py migrate your_app_name zero
```

Then, run the initial migration command:

```
$ python manage.py makemigrations your_app_name
```

You'll need to repeat this process for all apps in your project.

12.4. Solving Circular Dependencies

The prioritized solution for a circular dependency is to refactor your models such that the circular dependency no longer exists. This usually involves moving a field to another model or creating a new model to contain the cyclically-dependent fields.

If you simply can't refactor the models to remove the circular dependency, you can use South's `depends_on` feature to explicitly manage the migration order.

Despite these roadblocks, never lose sight of your capacity to learn from these setbacks. After all, the crux of advancement lies in manœuvring around obstacles. You are one step closer to mastering Django and South migrations. Remember, exploration is the heart of development —so keep exploring, keep building, and keep learning.

Chapter 13. Securing the Future: Best Practices for Sustainable Django Migrations

Django's migration system was developed to help developers make changes to their database schemas without having to worry about the tedious or error-prone aspects of manual SQL scripting. Nevertheless, to maximize it for scalability and sustainability, following strict best practices becomes absolutely non-negotiable.

The key to creating a sustainable migration plan is to stage changes thoughtfully and adopt alterations iterative in nature, facilitating smooth transitioning between application versions. This chapter focuses on some tenets to enforce this goal, ensuring the health of your database application over time.

13.1. Understanding Django Migration Files

Every Django migration file is an essential artifact of the state of your app at a given point in time. Django migrations are nothing more than Python files, each containing a subclass of `django.db.migrations.Migration`. They have a unique name and contain a list of changes to implement in the database schema. Each migration links to its predecessor, giving you an unbroken chain of schema evolution.

In general, migration files include two key components: the `dependencies` class variable, and a list of `operations` to perform. They're usually created using Django's `makemigrations` command, which automatically generates the necessary Python file based on detected changes in the models.

Understanding how to interpret and manipulate these files will enhance your control over your database schema and enable you to write efficient, sustainable migrations.

13.2. Developing Forward Thinking Migrations

Consideration for the future of the project should be paramount when designing database alterations. The primary objective should be a smooth upgrade experience for end-users and fellow developers.

To ensure your migrations are forward-thinking, try to design your models in a manner that they require fewer alterations down the line. For instance, when considering foreign key additions, analyse whether they are absolutely necessary or if the same can be accomplished using existing relations. This reduces the number of future migrations and assists in maintaining a clean and logical database schema.

Moreover, in any situation where breaking changes are necessary, they should be divided into several phased migrations, rather than one large, 'destructive' migration. The goal should be to make every migration process reversible, without creating bottlenecks or pain points.

13.3. Streamlining Django Migrations in Teams

Creating a simple, streamlined workflow for migrations is crucial when working with a team of developers. It helps to avoid conflicting migrations, which often result in broken applications and inefficient development cycles.

When collaborating on a Django project, it's critical to maintain clear lines of communication when applying migrations. Every team member should be aware before any migrations are made, so they can update their version of the codebase and prevent inconsistencies.

One good practice is to have a centralized system for applying migrations to shared development environments. Migrations should not be applied ad-hoc by individual developers. Instead, they should be reviewed and rolled out according to a set schedule.

13.4. Applying Migrations in a Production Environment

Flawlessly executing migrations in a production environment is an art with profound implications. Although Django provides robust mechanisms, such as migration squashing and backward migrations, for reducing the complexities of managing migrations, a mindfulness of good migration hygiene remains indispensable.

Provided you've adhered to the tenets outlined above, your migrations should execute smoothly. However, an extra caution should always be exercised before deployments to production. A best practice is to simulate the migration process in a staging environment that mirrors the live setup. This helps in identifying potential issues that might occur during the actual migration, while not impacting your users.

If you must apply migrations that may cause downtime (such as table alteration operations), it's recommended to plan outages for periods when user activity is at its lowest. The Plan-Carry-Verify-React approach ensures that you've planned the migration, carried it out, verified its success, and have an established plan of reaction in case of any untoward incidents.

13.5. Refactoring and Optimizing Migrations

Over time, the number of migrations in your Django project can stack, leading to slower test runs and making database setups a tedious affair. Django offers a feature known as "migration squashing" to combat this.

Migration squashing is the process of condensing many separate migrations into a single one. Django accomplishes this by squashing every operation into one migration operation, reducing the number of SQL commands and boosting performance.

However, squashing is not a panacea and must be carefully performed. Always test a squashed migration before deployment to avoid breaking your application.

In the end, maintaining a healthy migration practice in Django is less about the framework's mechanisms and more about a disciplined approach to handling database schema changes. Creating a sustainable migration plan is crucial, as is executing it in a controlled manner that keeps stakeholders informed and ensures smooth application evolution. Remember, the database is the heart of the software application, and ensuring its health will invariably lead to longer and more fruitful application lifetimes.